ISBN: 978-1-907526-03-9

DEDICATION

For Thine is the Kingdom, the Power and
the Glory. Forever and ever. Amen
Jesus loves the little children.

Prince Save

.\

CONTENTS

Prince Save

Prince Save

ACKNOWLEDGEMENTS

Thanking God for inspiration unto all good works. It is the zeal of the Lord that sees projects to completion. Thanking Toby for helping with editing and providing the original plot those many moons ago. To my illustrious and patient Illustrator, Richard Uff a big thank you.

For Toby's kindness and time for being the silent co-Author and fresh eye when it needed proofreading.

For all those Readers who purchased the first edition, thanks a lot! Keep your bright minds forever young. I appreciate early purchasers so much that you are all entitled to a discount if you can produce your original copy. To all those who provided professional support, near and far, thank you for accommodating me.

I appreciate every resource that has been placed at my disposal, including Amazon's KDP and other self-publishing gurus whose contribution has helped me improve with each publication. I am most grateful for your continued support. Please keep on praying, it makes a difference. Thank you ever so much for sharing the links and telling friends about the books too. Keep shining. Be blessed. You are a blessing.

DISCLAIMER

All errors are mine. This book is a work of
fiction and none of the characters are based
on persons known to me.

There is room for improvement and any feedback
will be appreciated.

Prince Save

Prince Save

DREAMING OF ROBOT LAND

I dream of robot land
A robotic mound of plastic
I dream of robot football land
That God likes football too

Almighty Saviour
Is the best goalkeeper
Saving all the balls
For his home team

Just visit robot football
And watch me play
I am also dreaming of mummy
Screaming "Toby do not kick that ball through
my house!"

I also dream of school
My friends and my class
And having fun learning
But I love going on school trips

Prince Save

I think we have short play time
And I dream of football club too
Do not tell Mum because she says,
School is for learning not playing

Sometimes I dream of owning a quad bike
Racing down the beach
But it is just a dream because Mum
Will not allow me to own a motorbike

Not at 7 but when I take a hike
From under her roof
So, I must continue to dream
Until I am older

Because in my dream
I have my own roof
Everybody dreams
My heroes and superheroes

My house will have a zero plastic robot park
And my supermarket will have people
My dream is not that dark
Because people must be preferred over robots

Martin Luther King had a dream

Prince Save

And President Obama
Had dreams from his Father
Abraham Lincoln made us all dream

They are all from America
Madiba walked to freedom
But he was from South Africa
What do I dream in England?

That it does not become robot land
Or zombie land
Or war land
But talent land

Robots cannot dream
Mum says great purpose begins with a dream
She likes Sir Tim Berners Lee
She loves Churchill best

With Big Ben chiming
And me riding the London Eye
Great men built this land
Greater ones will build it better

Robots and drones
They all have their uses

Prince Save

But whether we should have more or less robots
Depends on your dream

.

Prince Save

CHAPTER 1

Prince Save to the Rescue

Once upon a time there lived a Prince called Prince Save. Prince Save only had a Queen and a King but had not yet gotten a Princess. So, he lived at his parents' castle, Pearly Dew. In the Kingdom of Gladtidings.

A distant cousin of the royal family called, Goode Lee also had a Son, called Fisto Bratly. He also lived in Gladtidings. But his castle was a bit in the outskirts at a place called Devols Vamp. He was a very nasty villain who always wore black robes. His sole desire was to rule the Kingdom of Gladtidings. Not by fair but by foul, come what may! Fisto Bratly prioritised his ill intent from childhood and refused to learn anything in School. But he enjoyed many languages and magic. This was an unspoken secret. He was very very very good and so he was left to his own devices.

However, now as an adult he was not just a naughty prankster but with his spells, he was creating havoc! He made the lives of those loyal to their King and Queen totally miserable. He could travel anywhere he imagined without using a horse or an airplane. Now that we have drones, who knows, maybe that is what he had. Or he teleported like Dr Who. He would even dream about all the people lying prostrate on the ground for his horse to ride on their backs. Not even because he cared about keeping her hoofs clean. Rather, he enjoyed seeing people hurt.

Prince Save

Prince Save on the other hand, wore very nice blue boots and a green, yellow and red gown everywhere he went. People recognised him and would wave whenever he was passing. Cats purred at him. Dogs jumped all over him. Stallions neighed with pride. Even the sun would shine when he was out in the bitterest cold of winter! No matter how he dressed, blue or yellow or red or green were part of his attire.

His favourite colour was blue so he was also a Chelsea supporter. A yellow fabric shining very much like yellow gold, covered the sheath holding his sword. It was real gold you see, but it was best to leave people guessing when it came to his personal safety. This was top secret and not even Fisto Bratly, was allowed to know. No way! The true extent of wealth within the royal household was to remain a secret.

Prince Save

As you can imagine, this left Fisto Bratly fuming time and time again. The sole reason why he wanted power was to support his frivolous and reckless lifestyle. Especially since villains always try to invade the Kingdom to raid its wealth and treasures. Fisto Bratly was greedy and wanted everything just for himself. Yet, he dreaded being a victim of crime. He thought that the world was becoming more dangerous because he had been getting away with dodgy activities without being caught by the Police. He failed to realise that the dangerous world was purely down to an increase in crimes committed by people just like him.

Traditions of Gladtidings

Aside from security reasons the people of Gladtidings were very humble. They frowned on bragging and stayed away from new money. Those with newly acquired wealth with the uncouth habit of boasting were considered very unchristian. They sometimes had a talk with the Priest about being sorry for making those who did not have as much feel bad. But that did not stop Fisto Bratly. Aside from money, he did not care much about anything. Especially God or hurting others.

Prince Save meanwhile, never even left his room without his sword of supernatural powers. As heir to the throne of Gladtidings, his father, King Noble, had given it to him upon attaining the age of adolescence. It quickly became his prized possession.

This was a tradition because the Wise Greys of Gladtidings, closely watched the aging royals. It was their duty as custodians of tradition, to ensure that all royals stuck to tradition. Since one of their ancestry had gone bitter, angry and deranged in old age. They concluded that it was because his predecessor had not handed down the sword in good time.

Prince Save

When Prince Save received his sword from his father, he was warned to never answer any questions about his sword. He understood then that it was time for him to start courting his future bride. He had already been trained about being wary of Delilahs. In case he was asked how he managed to keep himself and Gladtidings safe, he would simply respond, 'I put my trust in God's Holy Word'.

The world was baffled because they had

bombs, chemical weapons, missiles, biological weapons, nuclear weapons, guns and all manner of deadly ammunition to defend themselves or assault the enemy. Due to this fascination, they never rejected invitations to banquets at Pearly Dew castle. Where they were all given special keys by guards at the gates to permit them entry.

Nothing penetrates Gladtidings. Even those marketing weapons cannot have audience at the Castle. This invisible shield would not allow anyone with evil ammunition or intent to enter the Kingdom. Even ownership of cake knives required registration in Gladtidings. It has been told that their enemies have marched around the Kingdom thousands of years but always missed the entrance.

Prince Save and Gladtidings officials on the other hand frequently travel on official business. Their safe return is always guaranteed, through the gates. Spies have tried to capture servants and citizens but it was futile. Most gave up and thought such a kingdom was a fable. Or dismissed it as wizardry and trickery because they did not serve the same God as the people of Gladtidings.

Plot to overthrow and supplant

Eventually, Fisto Bratly schemed with some notorious and dangerous bandits. Former allies who had gone rogue when their kingdoms were ruined, also joined him. They were insane with jealousy and greed. They schemed to kidnap a genuine royal because a true royal knows everything. They intended to win his trust to destroy Gladtidings and where very cunning about it.

First, they had to weaken the Kingdom and change its people. They found this process way too slow. Even though they used technology. In the end, they had to engage other not so subtle methods. Although some of them had genuine grievances, the King's Chancellors were unaware of this. And pretty soon the disgruntled agreed that injustice was justice denied and resorted to mob justice instead. Rejecting the rule of law, they became intoxicated with malice, corruption, violence and destruction.

Task Force

Ensuing events deeply troubled the nobles and King. When bad things started happening in his Kingdom, people were falling ill constantly. The Priests prayed but healing did not last long before they fell sick again. This was due to toxic and obnoxious substance which King Noble knew could not have entered his kingdom. It was a great mystery. People started to complain of stress at work because some people had started doing terrible things to each other.

During this period, King Noble never suspected that Fisto Bratly knew anything about it. Nor that he was a part of it. But his fathers had thought him that dividing the Kingdom would start decay. So, he knew that the Gladtidings was being divided and had to swing into action swiftly but cautiously. Not sure of who to trust.

His Task Force had reported that all those who craved power were helping Fisto Bratly to destroy the kingdom so that they could rule and enrich themselves. Apparently, they felt leadership was about enjoyment and it was their turn to enjoy. Which they believed would happen by crowning Fisto Bratly as King. They had no plan. No policy. No direction whatsoever except booze, party, drugs and sex. Fisto Bratly did not even sense that he was in danger of being betrayed and locked up by his

Prince Save

accomplices.

The apple fell far from the tree

The kind people of Gladtidings had made his Father feel so welcome that he decided to settle in Gladtidings and ended up starting his own family. They opened the first Church School for children. He felt so much love that he gave so much more kindness in return.

Aside from raising and training Clergy and Missionaries. He would repair anything and he felt very much like one of them. He had only kind thoughts and wept each time rogues from surrounding places invaded their land. Even those seriously sick from injury, defending the kingdom were healed after the laying of hands.

Nevertheless, the destruction and chaos of those invasions always found them

17

unprepared and left them rebuilding
Gladtidings all over again. At much
expense of time and money. His memories
were always tinged with much sadness and
regret for the departure of those friends and
family members who migrated to more
secure lands, as a result.

It was on a Sunday at Church that he had
announced to the congregation that God
had given him a vision to invent the
invisible shield. We may never know how it
was built because there were only 5 builders
who only worked late at night when the
people of Gladtidings were asleep. To date,
nobody knows the identity of the 5th person.

Due to this background, good people never
suspected a thing. They just felt something
was odd and kept inventing antidotes to
counter everything. The Christians prayed
even harder. Although they feared Fisto
Bratly because he used sorcery to

manipulate his way. Whereas his Father used prayers when he was alive. Brave people with knowledge of their history, remained loyal to their King.

But none of them knew just how desperate Fisto Bratly had become. He grew very impatient and very unhappy by the day.

In fact, he did not realise how lucky he was that Historians were wise, kind men, who actually never revealed that he was not of royal blood. Perhaps it would have helped if he knew that he was the adopted son of a loyal hero who stumbled upon their Land. Although he knew about his late Father's heroics, he never wanted to be like his Father. Alas! He thought his Father was a fool because he always insisted on him doing the right thing.

CHAPTER 2

Fisto Bratly knew he was not as popular as Prince Save so he grew obsessively jealous. Especially when he realised that Princess Primrose of Truly Kingdom liked Prince Save. You see, although Fisto Bratly was almost as rich as the King, he was happier coveting, cheating and amassing wealth that belonged to others.

Princess Primrose

In those days, sons inherited more from their Father but flaunting his possessions did not even make Princess Primrose like his heart. He showered her with gifts which she consistently returned. She had made it quite clear that she preferred the future King. She felt he was wise, kind and gentle. He loved everybody, even Fisto Bratly. Which she sensed was down to him not

Prince Save

knowing the evil schemes, that Fisto Bratly was capable of. Prince Save simply avoided spending too much time with him and she wished she knew the reason.

Prince Save

Princess Primrose was the most beautiful Princess in the entire world. Not particularly because she had the finest clothes or bone structure but she had her graces. She had a gorgeous smile and a very kind heart. Princess Primrose was ever so tender hearted with a beautiful singing voice that everyone admired. All who met her simply gushed with affection. Not even the maids or those banished would say an unkind word about her. If anything was ever hurtful, she would cry in secret so no one ever bothered being mean to her. It would be futile because it seemed nothing could prevent her from being happy. All she demanded from her friends was that they would always be truthful. From childhood when they would play at School, Prince Save just loved gazing into her big round eyes.

Prince Save

Courting Princess Primrose

Now, both Fisto Bratly and Prince Save liked Princess Primrose. Even though she was of Truly Kingdom. It meant marrying an outsider even though her father was a very powerful ally of King Noble.

Meanwhile, her father, King Valour, only had 2 daughters whom he wanted to fortify before his death. They called him King Valour because Truly Kingdom was the only land that had never been invaded by rogues and bandits. He was so wild, that he would order his cavalry to assault or ambush anyone at the hint of war. Although he had trained both daughters to be warriors, he always felt that Princess Primrose was too soft to take tough decisions.

But he loved both of his daughters equally. In fact, he secretly wished that he was as free as Princess Primrose.

Princess Primrose owned only 3 horses. But she rescued and kept many unclaimed stray animals. Everyone thought she would be a Veterinary Doctor, like her Mother. People always consulted or visited her when animals went missing. Everyone knew she loved animals and rumour had it that animals throughout Truly Kingdom and beyond knew her because she mastered animal language. She was also known to have the cure for all animal complaints. Her Chef worried so much about her because she would sometimes miss mealtimes when preoccupied with caring for her animal friends or strays.

Fisto Bratly on a rampage

Prince Save also had a horse called Power, whom he loved very much. Power was the leader of the Animal Kingdom. She always told Prince Save everything she heard. She was so loyal, that King Noble declared that the only horses fit for members of the royal family must be of her pedigree. She loved Prince Save from the day that she was born. Power had told all the animals that he was kind and fair. Even the animal kingdom approved of Prince Save as future King.

One day, Fisto Bratly, who was very furious, stole Prince Save's sword and shield. He went to Princess Primrose's Palace stables and used the sword to slaughter all of Princess Primrose's pets and horses. Except a gerbil called Millet, who escaped.

Fisto Bratly then snuck into Princess Primrose's upstairs study at the castle. Having been smeared with horrific blood on the sword and shield and his boots. Princess Primrose was so mortified she called immediately "Guard!" Then she remembered that Fisto Bratly had convinced her to send her guards over to his Office quarters for training. Perplexed, she listened as he tried to explain that it was not human but animal blood. He explained that he had found the sword after scaring off someone looking like Prince Save. Who fled away from the horrific scene at the stables. Princess Primrose was very upset. So Fisto Bratly feigned sadness as he tried to comfort her. By then, his mind was already miles away too deep into his plots and schemes to understand the true horror of his actions.

Princess Primrose had suspected immediately that something was fishy, when he avoided her questions. Instead, he tried convincing her to send King Valour's Army to wage war on the Kingdom of Gladtidings. Princess Primrose had asked to speak with Prince Save first. So Fisto Bratly left her alone, promising to fetch her guards and send for Prince Save.

Prince Save

Meanwhile, Fisto Bratly was not yet done with hatching his dubious plots against Prince Save. Upon arrival at his old, dirty castle, he was fuming because Princess Primrose had refused to have war declared against his perceived rival. His obsession with the royal household had no boundaries. Feeling that he had not gone far enough, he got his book of spells out and conjured up a concoction to wipe out Prince Save. He shaved and had a wash for the first time in months. Feeling well groomed, he thought maybe this time, Princess Primrose would welcome him warmly.

Meanwhile, Millet had escaped to Power's stable and told her what happened. Power summoned the Council of animals and they decided to trust Prince Save. Seeing he had earlier reported to Power that his sword went missing. They narrated everything

Prince Save

that had happened at Truly Kingdom. They told him his life was in danger. Likewise, Princess Primrose, who was now under siege. They feared he could give her one of his potions to force her to fall in love with him.

Prince Save needed no more convincing. Up on Power he mounted, with Millet in his pocket. They raced to Princess Primrose's Castle. All the time, he was wondering which hedge of safety, Fisto Bratly penetrated in order to access his sword. While Parrott the Messenger, rushed around the royal household and the Kingdom of Gladtidings alerting, animals of the security breach.

CHAPTER 3

Meanwhile Fisto Bratly was waiting because he had convinced Princess Primrose to drink a warm drink to soothe her. So, he was confident that he had left her sleeping. He left the key outside her bedroom door and stayed on guard at the entrance.

When they arrived at Princess Primrose's castle, Prince Save noticed that Millet had jumped off because he was hungry and looking for cheese. Millet found his meal and quickly nibbled on it because he knew that Prince Save needed his help.

Millet is a hero

On his return, Power whispered quietly to her nice little friend. And off he scurried, down the corridor being guarded by Fisto Bratly. He could see in the dark and was sure of the location of Princess Primrose's bedroom.

He found her sitting up in bed, sobbing. Millet told her everything about what he had witnessed. How Fisto Bratly was the villain. She said that she knew because she had seen him pour a potion into her drink. Which she had pretended to drink. She was now desperately scared about the hopelessness of her situation and worried about Prince Save. She was sure that Fisto Bratly had lost his mind. Millet told her not to worry because Prince Save and Power were safe and had come to her rescue.

Prince Save is captured

Little did they know that whilst they were chatting, Fisto Bratly's guards had arrived and arrested Prince Save and Power. Prince Save had not quite understood the value of his missing sword until they were thrown in prison with no chance of escape at Devols Vamp. They had then returned to inform, and fetch Fisto Bratly because they were very proud of themselves.

They were exactly like Fisto Bratly, with no real friends. No one approved of the sinister work they did for Fisto Bratly. This meant that their plan was successful for the removal of King Noble. As without an heir, there would be no throne.

Upon arriving at Devols Vamp, Fisto Bratly used his wicked magic and turned Power and Prince Save into figurines. He then had them placed in a glass cabinet where he intended to keep them as deaf and dumb pets on display. Just in case he brought Princess Primrose for a visit and they tried to speak to her.

As part of his plan, he already had contractors renovating his castle in anticipation of her royal visit.

Fisto Bratly was very pleased with himself. He even gave his guards enough money to take the rest of the day off to drink themselves silly. He then returned to Truly Kingdom, to give Princess Primrose's Chef instructions for dinner before sending Chef home for the rest of the week.

A Miraculous Escape

After that, he returned home to Devols Vamp for a strong drink. He continued his double life working in Gladtidings Kingdom as if nothing had happened. First, he needed to win Princess Primrose before his fellow conspirators could surface.

He visited her daily and made sure she was fed and the other side of the Castle were none the wiser.

Prince Save

One evening, he arrived home to find his Contractors had finished renovating Devols Vamp. He was quite happy. He had a good wash. Dressed up smartly without his black robe before making his way swiftly to wake up Princess Primrose. Leaving a trail of potent cologne wafting behind him. He failed to notice that the door was ajar, until he found that her bed was empty. He almost fainted in shock!

Princess Primrose and Millet had escaped from the castle when they heard the commotion with the guards, as they fetched Fisto Bratley. Millet had followed them safely to Devols Vamp when he realised that Prince Save and Power were captured. He returned to meet Princess Primrose at a cottage where she was hiding. They decided to wait for Fisto Bratly to finish taking his bath before attempting to rescue Prince Save and Power. Devols Vamp was full of laser sensors and death traps for protection from intruders. He could easily press command buttons from his bathroom to have them trapped. They made their move once they were sure that he was halfway to Princess Primrose's castle.

They found Prince Save and Power in the cabinet because they were still glowing from the warmth of the blood that had been flowing through their veins. Princess Primrose opened the cabinet and picked up Prince Save. She was in tears because she was terribly sad. Her teardrop touched Prince Save whilst she held him. Suddenly the spell was broken. He felt heavier and she noticed that he was growing bigger and his voice recovered.

Soon he started changing and asked to be set down on the floor. She was so happy to hear him speak, that, she gave him a long kiss. While they were kissing, he grew taller and taller until she realised that he was now

lifting her.

Millet and Power were so excited that they started singing and dancing in celebration. They enjoyed themselves so much. Joining in the fun and laughter because they had solved this problem without going to war. Millet forgot Power was a horse when he kissed her.

Meanwhile, Prince Save's parents had sent guards to Princess Primrose's castle. They immediately arrested Fisto Bratly upon finding him alone weeping on her bedroom floor. He was so miserable, his answers to their questions were unintelligible. They led him immediately to King Noble, where he confessed absolutely everything. And was then bundled off to a cell to await trial.

Justice served

All of his accomplices were then arrested

and tried. But the opportunists among them, who were first time offenders and unaware of the full extent of their crimes, were given a second chance. They received a fine and a sentence to attend mental health assessments; citizen and behavioural classes.

The rest, depending on the extent of their involvement, either received custodial sentences or home imprisonment. Whilst the ringleaders were exiled to Bad People country, along with Fisto Bratly.

Bad people country

All the evil people in the world live together in Bad People country. Where their obsession was doing evil things to hurt each other. And that is where all banished criminals were permitted to stay because they refused to change. Apparently Fisto Bratly is now a very crooked fly that walks

36

with the help of a cane, instead of flying. Having met his match of evil person in bad people country who conjured up a bigger spell. O how he regrets his actions! Now that he has been banished and cannot even fly, it may be a bit too late. The King's Chancellors never visit those parts.

A royal wedding

Prince Save and Princess Primrose loved each other so much that, they had a joint wedding with Millet and Power. This took place the following week, after all the arrests and trial.

It was the biggest wedding in the Kingdom of Gladtidings. Besides, the only way they could ever get out of Devols Vamp was by the power of true love. They were happy forever couples indeed! They went on to have many beautiful, brave and kind children whose identities were kept secret.

37

Prince Save

As is now the tradition to safeguard their future. With the kind wise men who never age or die, watching very closely to see whether aging would cause either their parents to be demented or deranged. Whereby they would swiftly prescribe the best treatment because once progressed, it caused irreversible harm.

One day, Prince Save and Princess Primrose might be the ones to break that spell. For, if left unchecked, they end up hurting their own children. But that is a different story.

Prince Save

♫♫≈≈≈≈≈≈≈≈≈≈≈♫♫
Prince Save was wiser than Samson

He picked Primrose

Not Delilah

Nowadays there are all sorts of risks

From rogues

Zombies

Terrorists

And pirates

Holding nations to ransom

Or worse

What use is an election

Unless we see more good

Than bad

But there is never victory in evil

Prince Save

Afterall, where would we be without goodwill

And genuine people to make our world wholesome

To enjoy time with our animal friends

Who know more about good character

Fairness and doing the right thing

So please don't clip their wings

Don't harness their potential

Do the right thing

Be sure to look after your best friends

And be kind to your animal friends

For no one in their right mind

Will repay good for evil

God is the fairest Judge
♫♫≈≈≈≈≈≈≈≈≈≈≈♫♫

Prince Save

Prince Save

MY CHRISTMAS SONG

Blessed be the Lord God of Israel
For He hath visited and redeemed His
people
For unto us is born today
In the City of David
A Saviour

Prince Save

From a lowly stable
In Bethlehem
Jesus the son of Man
Joseph the Nazarene
Yet divine

A Wonderful Counsellor
A Messiah King
A King of Kings
Angel Gabriel and a multitude of heavenly
hosts
Hailed His royal birth

This too shall be my worship
For Baby Jesus
The Christ
I bring my gold frankincense and myrrh
His praise to sing

All our Christmas joy
Carols and anthem
We raise because He is worthy
Rejoice He is here

Prince Save

His love so bright it casts out fear

His name is Emmanuel
Meaning God is with us
For He came as promised
Let us celebrate and extol
This King so true

The Prince of Peace
Also is his name
For He brings peace goodwill to all men
The gift of eternal life
To them that will receive Him

He is faithful
His people will never be forsaken
His covenant will always be remembered
That He would grant unto His joint heirs
Deliverance out of the hand of our
enemies

Living in holiness and righteousness before
Him

Prince Save

We choose all the days of our lives
To give glory to God in the Highest
And on earth peace
Life in its abundance

Truth and grace
Are born today
Thank you for bringing hope
And the salvation of God for mankind
Happy birthday King Jesus

Prince Save

Prince Save

ABOUT THE AUTHOR

The Author uses Sharon Rose as her pseudonym. Good Friday was created as part of a trilogy and it is followed by Pirate Tommy and Prince Save. All of which were written in London in 2009.

Her works are underpinned by her Christian belief and does not refrain from quoting the Bible. Normally referenced as a yardstick for societal values and morals; or a source of joy, peace, liberty, inspiration, hope, information, knowledge and even entertainment.

Prince Save was first printed with Toby as Author and stick characters drawn by him, in Toby's KS1 & KS2 Stuff. It was a project created to immortalise his schoolwork from KS1 & KS2.

The Author now lives in Walsall with Toby. Having been on numerous 'adventures' in London, Uganda and The Gambia. Which has now inspired material for books for all age groups.

The Author has a solid legal background training, adjudicating, supporting in Secretarial capacity, proofreading, research and in a paralegal role. Currently looking forward to resuming her LLM studies with the BPP. She most recently worked as a Warehouse Operator and Warehouse Associate.

Prince Save

Printed in Great Britain
by Amazon

64137794R00033